A Drop In The Bucket

I0192163

_____
Name

_____
Date

Wine to Water Project

_____
Location

A Drop In The Bucket is your personal workbook. Here you will transfer your thoughts, feelings, ideas, prayers and dreams into words.

A Drop In The Bucket

Copyright © 2017

ISBN: 978-1-935256-63-2

Ledge Press
PO Box 1652
Boone, NC 28607
ledgepress@gmail.com

v 4/2017

Hello!

We are excited that you have chosen to serve with Wine To Water as an international volunteer! This is going to be a great experience with much learning and adventure around every corner. If you're reading this, you have already completed most, if not all, of the pre-trip requirements, so congratulations! Now, it's time to start preparing for your journey.

The purpose of a service trip is to give volunteers an opportunity to participate in one piece of the long-term process of learning about the water crisis, engaging with the culture, and serving in community around the world.

Although this experience will be fun, Wine To Water service trips are not a vacation. We expect you to come ready to serve, get your hands dirty, and work hard for the duration of the trip. Your tasks will include community development and water projects, and you will be working directly with our team throughout your service experience. It's important to keep in mind that you are not a superhero flying into these villages to save lives, but by working alongside locals and building relationships, you are assisting in providing sustainable clean water and educational resources to those in need.

Different is...Different

As an international traveler, there is a lot to consider before boarding your flight. The first thing to keep in mind is that you are about to enter into a completely different culture than what you may be used to. Different doesn't mean bad or wrong, it simply means different. You will experience different languages, different foods, different environments and different customs. It's important to remember that you're a visitor. We ask that you be flexible, maintain a positive attitude as you experience new things, and keep an open mind. Many times the hosts and nationals will do things differently than Westerners, and it's important to submit to their leadership, even if you do not fully understand the reasoning behind it.

This workbook is a resource for you to use to record your thoughts, feelings, and experiences throughout the trip. I hope it will help your trip become an unforgettable experience that motivates you to continue serving in community.

I am so excited that you have decided to join us in the field. Your trip is going to be a fun, action-packed, humbling adventure. I hope that this workbook is a helpful tool for you to use now, during your trip, and even after you return home.

Thank you for being willing to serve, for getting out of your comfort zone, for raising money to provide clean water around the world, and for your willingness to serve others. Welcome to the Wine To Water community!

Cheers,
Lisa Merritt, Volunteer Programs Director

Our Mission

Wine To Water is committed to serving in community to provide clean water to those in need.

About Wine To Water
Wine To Water's US staff shares a passion for providing clean water to folks in need. Our passion unites us and brings us joy as we work with our international teams. Wine To Water has worked in twenty-five countries, twelve of which are ongoing projects. We find it a privilege to work within a global community as we all work hard to fight this epidemic together.

What We Do
Each program is unique, but the common theme is that we focus on relationships wherever we work. We develop leaders in the community and work side by side with them on proper water and sanitation methods to promote sustainability. Our work empowers the local community to meet their ongoing needs.

How We Began
Doc Hendley is the Founder and International President of Wine To Water. In 2003 he dreamed up the concept of the organization while bartending and playing music in nightclubs around Raleigh, North Carolina. The first fundraiser was held in January, 2004 and by August of that year, Doc was living in Darfur, Sudan installing water systems for victims of the government-supported

genocide. When Doc returned home in August, 2005, the haunting memories of what he had seen in Darfur drove him to continue building the organization he had started two years earlier.

In 2007, Wine To Water became an official 501(c)3 nonprofit. In 2009, Doc and the work of the Wine To Water team was recognized by the CNN Heroes program, launching the organization's efforts globally. Doc's dream, and the goal of Wine To Water, is to serve in community to provide clean water to those in need.

With every project, the common thread in our work is ensuring that the implemented water solution meets the needs and resources specific to the local community. Our methods include shallow and deep wells, well repairs, ceramic water filters, biosand filters, Sawyer PointONE filters, and rainwater harvest tanks. We also improve sanitation by constructing latrines where needed and providing hygiene education. We use local materials whenever possible and are constantly striving to implement the most effective solutions for each project.

Where We Work
Wine To Water has supported water projects in 25 countries: Belize, the Democratic Republic of Congo (DRC), Dominican Republic, Costa Rica, Cambodia, Colombia, Brazil, Ecuador, Ethiopia, Guatemala, Haiti, Honduras, India, Kenya, Nepal, Peru, Philippines, South Africa, Sri Lanka, Sudan, Syria, Uganda, United States, Vietnam, and Zimbabwe.

There are three stages to this journal, which reflect the three stages of your upcoming adventure.

The first stage is Preparation or **Pre-Trip**. During this stage you will be meeting with your team and preparing for the volunteer experience. You will be learning about the country and the people you will be serving. A few days prior to the launch of the trip, pull out your workbook. Listen. Read. Think. Pray. Record.

The second stage is **On the Ground**. It launches when your feet touch the ground in your host country. This will be an exciting and busy time. You will be "crowded" and your daily schedule filled with new experiences. This is the time you will have to be intentional in finding a time to slip away and be alone. During this time: Listen. Read. Think. Pray. Record.

The third stage is the **Post-Trip**. It begins when your feet touch the ground back in your home country. You will be enthusiastic about what you have just experienced and will want others to understand what you just went through. But, due to the cultural differences you will experience, being able to convey what you have seen and felt may be difficult. Don't worry, this is normal! Even so, we believe sharing your story with others is helpful in processing what you have experienced and been a part of. As you reflect on the memories of your trip, and sift through your "re-entry" emotions, you will begin to merge your recent adventure with the normal routines of being home. This is a critical time to capture what is passing through your mind and heart. In some small way, we hope that your experience of being on a Wine To Water service trip will have a positive impact on your daily habits. During this stage: Listen. Read. Think. Pray. Record.

Pre-Trip Questions

1. Who or what motivated you to participate in this trip?

2. What are you hoping to see or do on this trip?

3. What would you like to personally accomplish on this trip?

4. How can you prepare for this trip?

   Mentally?

   Physically?

   Spiritually?

5. Define the following concepts:

   Being Teachable

Being Respectful

Being Flexible

6. When you see a foreigner in your country, what do
    you expect from them? (Cultural norms? Language
    fluency? Ability to drive?)

7. How do you view and/or treat someone who is a
    foreigner in your country, city, and/or environment?

8. How do you hope you are treated by the locals as you enter into their world as a foreigner?

Daily Reflection: At the end of each day reflect on the following questions. As you reflect, jot down words that describe your day.

High—What was the highlight of your day? What was the most exciting, interesting, or energizing moment?

Low—What was the hardest part of your day? What was the most saddening, confusing, or frustrating moment for you?

Impact Image for the day. What image, picture, vision, mental or emotional photograph pops into your mind about today?

On the Ground

Day 1: Travel Day

One's destination is never a place but a new way of seeing things. — Henry Miller

Now to him who is able to do far more abundantly than all that we ask or think, according to the power at work within us...Christ Jesus. — Ephesians 3:20-21

1. What are you imagining the week ahead is going to look like?

2. What are your first impressions of the:

    Culture?

    People?

    Food?

    Community?

3. Now that you're in the field with your whole team, how do you anticipate "serving in community"? What does that look like to you?

Day 2: Orientation

The value of a man should be seen in what he gives and not in what he is able to receive. — Albert Einstein

So in everything, do to others what you would have them do to you, for this sums up the Law and the Prophets. — Matthew 7:12

1. What is the purpose of the Volunteer Program at Wine To Water?

The the purpose of volunteer program is to be one part of a long-term process of learning about the water crisis, engaging with the culture, and serving in community.

2. What is your purpose for this trip? Why are you here?

3. What are your personal goals for this trip? What do you want to accomplish by the end of the week?

4. Two years from now, what is one thing in your life and actions that you would like to be different as a result of this trip?

Day 3: The Contract

Alone we can do so little; together we can do so much.
— Helen Keller

A new commandment I give to you, that you love one another: just as I have loved you, you also are to love one another. By this all people will know that you are my disciples, if you have love for one another.
— John 13:34-35

High

Low

Impact Image

The Contract:
- Be Here Now
- Give 110%
- Challenge by Choice
- Choose Joy
- Love Covers All

1. Define the word community.

2. How does this community play out in your life at home?

3. How do you anticipate community playing out this week?

Day 4: Poverty

There are people in the world so hungry, that God cannot appear to them except in the form of bread. — Gandhi

Jesus said to them, I am the bread of life; whoever comes to me shall not hunger, and whoever believes in me shall never thirst. — John 6:35

High

Low

Impact Image

1. What are the five words or phrases that come to your mind when you think of poverty?

2. How do you define poverty? How would you go about alleviating it?
    How a person defines poverty is often related to how they believe it should be alleviated. For example:

    *   If you think poverty is a lack of knowledge, you may want to help educate the poor.
    *   If you think poverty is oppression by powerful people, you may want to work for social justice.
    *   If you think poverty is caused by personal sins or poor choices, you may want to evangelize and disciple the poor.
    *   If you think poverty is a lack of material resources, you may want to contribute money or goods to poor communities.

3. How do you think an impoverished person defines poverty?

4. Think back to a time when you have felt unaccepted, shamed, hopeless or inferior. What or who brought you out of those feelings?

5. How do you think poverty is affected by a close and loving community?

Day 5: Perspective

For what you see and hear depends a good deal on where you are standing; it also depends on what sort of person you are. — C.S. Lewis, The Magician's Nephew

So we have stopped evaluating others from a human point of view. At one time we thought of Christ merely from a human point of view. How differently we know him now! This means that anyone who belongs to Christ has become a new person. The old life is gone; a new life has begun! And all of this is a gift from God, who brought us back to himself through Christ. — 2 Corinthians 5:16-18

High

Low

Impact Image

1. Who are the poor? (How are we rich? How are we poor? How is this community rich? How are they poor?) Matthew 5:3

2. Helping or Hurting? Have you ever experienced this dynamic?

David Livermore, who has spent years studying cross-cultural engagement and short-term missions, shares a story that illustrates this dynamic. He and his wife, Linda, and their daughters were visiting Malaysia. After seeing a materially poor Malay father and daughter on the street, Livermore encouraged his own daughter to give the little girl a frog stuffed animal. "As we started to leave, the Malay father ordered his daughter to return the frog. We motioned that we didn't want it back, but he insisted. He began to raise his voice and grabbed the frog and handed it to me. As I began to talk with Linda about it we thought back to our home in the Chicago area. Though a beautiful house, our home was one of the more modest homes in our town. Linda asked, "'So how would you feel if one of the parents in the million-dollar homes near us suddenly walked up to our girls and started handing them gifts?'" All of a sudden I began to see this in a new light. I thought about how I would feel if some rich person started giving my girls unsolicited gifts in my presence. I'm quite capable of caring for them, thank you!" — Helping Without Hurting

3. What's something you are learning about how to engage with a community?

4. What are some ways you can engage with a community in true humility?

Day 6: Serve

You must be the change you wish to see in the world. —
Mahatma Gandhi

...let the greatest among you become as the youngest,
and the leader as one who serves. — Luke 22:26

High

Low

Impact Image

1. When is it okay to give something to someone at no
    cost?

RELIEF, REHABILITATION, AND DEVELOPMENT

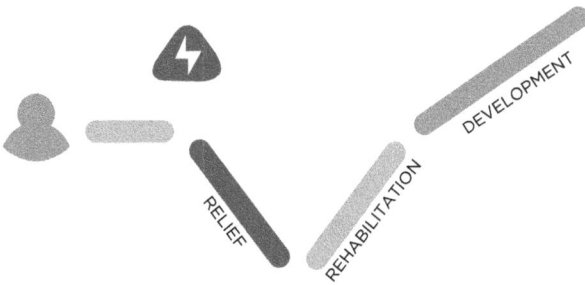

2. Think about the community here. Is the current need mostly for relief, rehabilitation, or development?

Relief—An effort to "stop the bleeding." It is the urgent and temporary provisions of emergency aid to reduce suffering from a natural or man-made crisis and it primarily utilizes a provider-receiver dynamic.

Rehabilitation—An effort to restore people back to their pre-crisis state after the initial bleeding has stopped, while also laying the basis for future development. In rehabilitation, people begin to contribute to improving their situation.

Development—Walking with people across time in ways that move all the people involved—both the "helpers" and the "helped"—closer to being in a right relationship with God, self, others, and the rest of creation than they were before. This involved people identifying their problems creating solutions, and implementing those solutions. Development is often referred to as "empowerment." It avoids "doing for" and focuses on "doing with."

3. What area does WTW primarily work in and why?

4. What does it mean to serve others?

5. What does it mean to be served? How does the trip shape this view?

Day 7: Change

If we are to go forward, we must go back and rediscover those precious values—that all reality hinges on moral foundations and that all reality has spiritual control.
— Martin Luther King, Jr.

And let us consider how to stir up one another to love and good works, not neglecting to meet together, as is the habit of some, but encouraging one another...
— Hebrews 10:24-25

High

Low

Impact Image

1. How did you spend your time today? Who did you interact with today?

2. The trip is almost over. So, what do you want to challenge yourself to do tomorrow?

3. People > Projects: What does this mean to you?

4. What is something you have learned from this community?

5. What are you learning about being a part of a community and working together?

Day 8: Living

If you can't fly then run, if you can't run, then walk, if you can't walk then crawl, but whatever you do you have to keep moving forward. — Martin Luther King, Jr.

Not that I have already obtained this or am already perfect, but I press on to make it my own, because Christ Jesus has made me his own...I press on toward the goal for the prize of the upward call of God in Christ Jesus. — Philippians 3:12-14

High

Low

Impact Image

1. How are you living out the contract (from Day 3 page 15)?

2. What are some ways you can continue the process of learning, serving, and engagement when you return home? For example, how can you:

   - Continue to support the work you are doing here?
   - Effectively alleviate poverty in your own community?
   - Serve your community back home?

Write down some ideas about where to begin. It might be people, places, organizations, churches, or other ideas.

3. Revisit your goals from the beginning of the week. Have these goals changed? If so, what are your new goals?

Day 9: Reorientation

If you want to identify me, ask me not where I live, or what I like to eat, or how I comb my hair, but ask me what I am living for, in detail, ask me what I think is keeping me from living fully for the thing I want to live for.
— Thomas Merton

Brothers, I do not consider that I have made it my own. But one thing I do: forgetting what lies behind and straining forward to what lies ahead, I press on toward the goal for the prize of the upward call of God in Christ.
— Philippians 2: 13-14

1. Write down two moments from your trip that had the most impact on you.

2. What was the most difficult part of the trip? What was the most saddening, confusing, or frustrating moment for you?

3. Think back to your first day. Have your first impressions changed?

About team members?

About the community?

4. Which part of the service trip is the most important? Why? (Pre-trip? In the Field? Post-trip?)

5. Mosaic Image – What part did you play this week? Why are you important?

6. How are you going to answer the question, "How was your trip?"

7. Was there a specific time during your trip that you felt your group become a community? Describe that moment.

8. John 6. Jesus feeds the 5,000 – What are your two small fish and five small barley loaves?

9. What is one practical/tangible/measurable thing that you are going to do or change when you get back home?

10. Now that it's the end of your trip, revisit what your purpose was on the first day and see if anything has changed.

What does it mean to live with purpose, or on purpose? How does this trip contribute to this thought?

Write a letter to yourself, and be sure to include:
- What did you experience?
- What did you learn?
- What are you going to do about it?
- Why are you important?

As we re-enter your normal world there are five phases of emotional adjustment that are common after an international experience. Use these stages and reflect upon them during the following days and weeks.

Possible Stages for Re-entry
The following stages mention the cycle you may go through emotionally as you re-enter your home world.

Fun (honeymoon). Sharing the stories. Re-living the adventure.

Flee (avoidance). May begin to feel alone. Many of your family and friends have not had this adventure and cannot relate to what you have gone through and what you are feeling.

Fight (anger, criticism). Emotionally begin to fight back. Feelings of how unfair our way of life is compare to what you have just experienced. Anger at others for not understanding.

Fit In (tolerance of differences). Survival. Acceptance and willing to acknowledge that others cannot know and experience what you feel. And acceptance of the idea that only when you experience something first-hand will you gain a surface understanding of what goes on in third world countries.

Forget. Yep. It begins to fade away.

OR

Fruitful (creative engagement). Finding ways to encourage others to share this same adventure you have had. Educating others and challenging others on the needs of the world, both spiritual needs and physical needs.

(Adapted from Lisa Espineli Chinn, Reentry Guide for Short Term Mission Leaders, Orlando: DeeperRoots Publications p. 14, used by permission of the author.)

Day 10: Travel Home

The best way to cheer yourself up is to try to cheer somebody else up. — Mark Twain

The generous will themselves be blessed, for they share food with the poor. — Proverbs 22:9

1. What are you looking forward to the most about being home?

2. How are you going to answer the question: How was your trip?

3. What are some of your fears as you go home?

4. Write down what you are

   Feeling

   Thinking

   Hoping

Post-Trip

I am only one, but still I am one. I cannot do everything, but still I can something; and because I cannot do everything, I will not refuse to do something I can do. — Helen Keller

And Jesus grew in wisdom and stature, and in favor with God and man. Luke 2:52

1. In what ways did the national hosts serve you and your team while you were on the ground? How does this relate to your culture back home?

2. How did your visit led to positive change in a materially poor community?

3. What are your commitments? Write down what you want to do in the next

   Two weeks

   Six months

   Year

4. Review your goals from Day 2: On The Ground. Are you still working on achieving those goals?

5. What are some obstacles preventing you from reaching your goals?

6. How will you overcome these obstacles?

7. What have I done to report back to those who supported and sent me?

8. How can I stay more connected to Wine To Water?

How Can I Stay Involved With Wine To Water?

Online

Now that you have made Wine To Water a part of your personal story, there are many different ways to stay engaged with the community.

1. Follow us on Facebook, Twitter and Instagram!

2. Make sure that you or your team leader has an appropriate email contact so that we can send you updates from the region and the Wine To Water community.

3. Check our website regularly for new stories and program developments.

4. Continue to send your thoughts, memories and notes to fieldnotes@winetowater.org. The journey doesn't end when you go home and neither does the story. What you have to share is important! Share it with the community!

Wine

Second, order some wine and share it with friends and family! This could be a wonderful chance to share some of your experiences from your trip. Or give a bottle as a gift to someone special. You can order wine online at: winetowater.org/wine

Fundraise

Third, consider fundraising for WTW in your area! You can create an online campaign or host an event, such as a wine tasting or walk for water. We have plenty of information to help you get started and point you in the direction you would like to take your campaign. Check out our website and start fundraising at: winetowater. org/fundraise

Chapters

Fourth, find or join a local chapter! We have Wine To Water chapters in cities across the country. Chapters are groups of like-minded people who work together as a local community to organize events, raise awareness about Wine To Water and serve on volunteer trips regularly. If you don't have a chapter in your area, consider starting one! winetowater.org/chapters

Just One Shift

Fifth, if you work in the service industry, you may be interested in our Just One Shift fundraising campaign. Just One Shift was originally designed around World Water Day for bartenders, servers, restaurants to give one shift of their earnings to help solve the water crisis, but we asked ourselves why stop there? Anyone can give a shift anytime of year—a birthday, a season, or a sacrifice to help join the cause! If you don't work in the service industry, consider creating your own creative Just One Shift! What is your ONE thing you are going to give to fight the water crisis with us?

Serve Again

Last, but certainly not least, start thinking about your next volunteer trip! Keep an eye on our schedule and invite your friends and family to join you! winetowater.org/serve

Appendix

Follow Up Thank You Letter

As you return home, you have several stories and people that have impacted your experience this past week. It's important to remember the people back home who supported and allowed you to have this experience. We suggest showing your appreciation to these folks by sending them a note. This note could include some stories and stats from your past week, how it's impacted you and the community, or just a simple thank you! It's a way for them to stay engaged with your experience after you return.

A quick and inexpensive way of thanking people is to download the "ink" app on your phone. In this app, you can send a quick postcard to someone by uploading a photo from the trip and typing out a little blurb.

Here is a sample letter:

Hey Robin,

Thanks so much for your support in allowing me to go serve in Nepal. It was an incredible experience and I'll have to tell you a story about this little boy, I met while I was there. Santosh stole my heart!! He was just one of the 600 children that received clean water for the first time this week—such a powerful moment to see the water come out of their new well. It reminds me to be thankful for all the blessings I have. I will be forever changed because of this trip and just wanted to thank you for allowing me to serve in this way.

Much love,

Lisa

Sample Field Note

A field note is just a snapshot from your perspective of an image or moment that has an impact on you. It doesn't have to be long, but just make sure it captures what you are seeing, doing, feeling, or experiencing. www.winetowater.org/stories

I've been back from Nepal for one week now and as I continue to look through pictures I feel my heart being tugged on and I'm filled with joy!

— Sarah McKee

It's the day before our first fundraising event, and I'm sorting through pictures of my trip to the Dominican Republic. I'm reflecting on my experience and what I want to communicate to our guests before my trip to Nepal. Walking through El Higuerito, I remember being struck by the relationships that were already formed between WTW and the community there. I want to see that emphasis at work again on my next trip, and I can't wait to carry that over into my own community, whatever that may look like.

— Robin White

In early September 2016, a volunteer team of 10 members, went to Nepal. We traveled to the Chitwan National Forest to work in the small community of Jhuwani. There was already a well in this community, but if you were part of the lower/untouchables caste, you had to wait your turn to be able to use the well.

A woman from the lower caste shared with us that she had to wait 4 hours everyday just to use the well, even if she got there first. Our WTW Nepal team, along with the volunteers, decided to dig a well on her side of the street for these folks. Imagine having 4 hours of freedom added to your day!
— Lisa Merritt

Wash Lesson Plan Tips & Sample Exercises
Handwashing: Keeping hands clean is one of the most important steps we can take to avoid getting sick and spreading germs to others. Many diseases and conditions are spread by not washing hands with soap and clean, running water. There are critical times when hand washing should be done. Ask the participants to list those times. Here are some examples: after defecation, after handling child feces or cleaning a child's anus, before preparing food, before feeding a child, before eating.

Optional interactive activity:
1. Put a small amount of loose glitter on your hands without the participants knowing. Use different colored glitter for different people.

2. Shake hands with everyone and ask them to shake hands and high five with each other as if they are meeting in the street or at a community gathering.
3. Ask the participants "What diseases can be passed between people when they shake hands?"

How To Wash Hands Thoroughly:

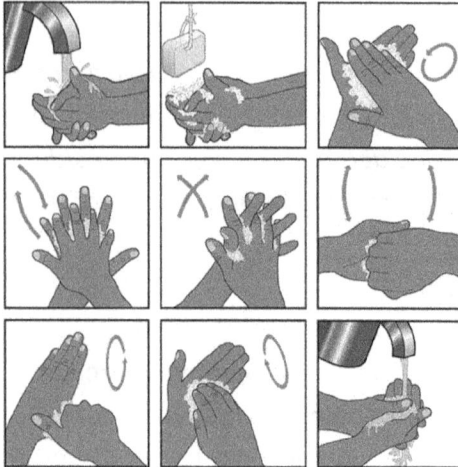

Sanitation: Basic sanitation hygienically separates excreta from human contact. Sanitation contributes to social, and economic development of the society. Improved sanitation also helps the environment.

Environmental sanitation: A broader definition of sanitation and tries to include all aspects which may affect human health and well-being. It typically includes excreta management, domestic wastewater management, stormwater drainage, solid waste management and vector control. As well, drinking water is sometimes included in the definition, as sustainable environmental sanitation cannot be planned and implemented in isolation from water supply.

Optional interactive activity: Have participants discuss different forms of contamination. You can refer to the poster below.

How Water Is Contaminated:

Latrine Cleanliness: When latrines are dirty it leads to people not wanting to use them which defeats the purpose of sustainable sanitation and can lead to transmittal of disease. The most common diseases include typhoid, dysentery, cholera, hepatitis A and E, shigellosis, giardiasis, cryptosporidiosis, ascariasis and hookworm.

Optional interactive activity: Ask participants to fill out the chart below with the appropriate needs of their private and community latrines.

ACTIVITY	HOW	FREQUENCY	WHY
Wash slab and toilet			
Tidy area around the latrine			
Wash door handles and lock			

Improved Sanitation

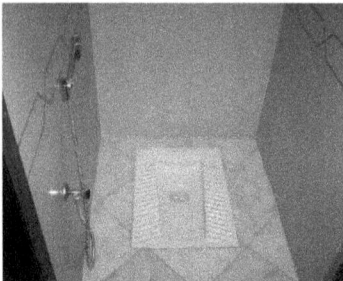

Unimproved Sanitation

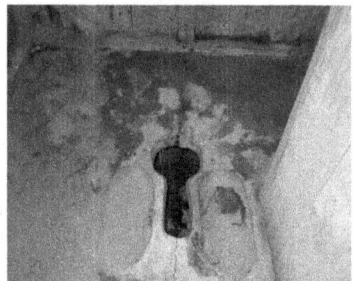

Menstrual Hygiene: Menstruation is the natural process of shedding the lining of a woman or adolescent girl's uterus. During menstruation, blood flows from the uterus and passes out of the body through the vagina. This process happens for 2-7 days every month as part of a normal menstrual cycle. Girls begin to menstruate usually between the ages of 9 and 14. Menstruation usually stops when a women is in her late 40s or early 50s, which is called menopause. A woman will menstruate for approximately 3,000 days during her lifetime. Having regular menstrual cycles is a sign that important parts of the female body are working normally. The menstrual cycle provides important body chemicals, called hormones, to keep women and girls healthy. It also prepares the body for pregnancy each month.

Reports have identified links between poor menstrual hygiene practices and the following health impacts in women and girls: rashes and irritations; urinary, vaginal and perineal infections; complications with reproduction and pregnancy, complications associated with female genital mutilation or cutting.

Challenges and barriers to proper menstrual sanitation are: lack of sanitary products, lack of water and soap for cleaning, lack of access to appropriate sanitation facilities, cultural and religious restrictions, shame and embarrassment, lack of information and awareness.

Optional interactive activity: Ask participants to brainstorm some solutions to the barriers and challenges. After 5 minutes, discuss the solutions with the large group.

Possible solutions: Ensure sanitary products and underwear are available, affordable, and easy to access. Provide access to water, sanitation and hygiene at home and in public places, like schools and work. Women and girls need somewhere safe and private to change their sanitary products; clean water and soap for washing their hands, bodies, and reusable cloths; and facilities for safely disposing of used sanitary products or a clean and well lit place to dry them if reusable. Provide factual information to girls and boys, men and women to counter negative customs and give positive support to women and girls. Offer education programs for teachers and school authorities, as well as sensitization for parents and wider communities.

*Images and activities taken from CAWST

Relevant Scriptures For The Week

Turning Water into Wine: John 2:1-11 NLT

The next day there was a wedding celebration in the village of Cana in Galilee. Jesus' mother was there, 2 and Jesus and his disciples were also invited to the celebration. 3 The wine supply ran out during the festivities, so Jesus' mother told him, "They have no more wine." 4 "Dear woman, that's not our problem," Jesus replied. "My time has not yet come." 5 But his mother told the servants, "Do whatever he tells you." 6 Standing nearby were six stone water jars, used for Jewish ceremonial washing. Each could hold twenty to thirty gallons. 7 Jesus told the servants, "Fill the jars with water." When the jars had been filled, 8 he said, "Now dip some out, and take it to the master of ceremonies." So the servants followed his instructions. 9 When the master of ceremonies tasted the water that was now wine, not knowing where it had come from (though, of course, the servants knew), he called the bridegroom over. 10 "A host always serves the best wine first," he said. "Then, when everyone has had a lot to drink, he brings out the less expensive wine. But you have kept the best until now!" 11 This miraculous sign at Cana in Galilee was the first time Jesus revealed his glory. And his disciples believed in him.

Importance of Water: Exodus 15:22

Then Moses led the people of Israel away from the Red Sea, and they moved out into the desert of Shur. They traveled in this desert for three days without finding any water.

Not to be served, but to serve: Matthew 20:26-28 NLT

26 But among you it will be different. Whoever wants to be a leader among you must be your servant, 27 and whoever wants to be first among you must become your slave. 28 For even the Son of Man came not to be served but to serve others and to give his life as a ransom for many.

Samaritan Woman at the Well: John 4:1-15 NLT

Jesus knew the Pharisees had heard that he was baptizing and making more disciples than John 2 (though Jesus himself didn't baptize them—his disciples did). 3 So he left Judea and returned to Galilee. 4 He had to go through Samaria on the way. 5 Eventually he came to the Samaritan village of Sychar, near the field that Jacob gave to his son Joseph. 6 Jacob's well was there; and Jesus, tired from the long walk, sat wearily beside the well about noontime. 7 Soon a Samaritan woman came to draw water, and Jesus said to her, "Please give me a drink." 8 He was alone at the time because his disciples had gone into the village to buy some food. 9 The woman was surprised, for Jews refuse to have anything to do with Samaritans. She said to Jesus, "You are a Jew, and I am a Samaritan woman. Why are you asking me for a drink?" 10 Jesus replied, "If you only knew the gift God has for you and who you are speaking to, you would ask me, and I would give you living water." 11 "But sir, you don't have a rope or a bucket," she said, "and this well is very deep. Where would you get this living water? 12 And besides, do you think you're greater than our ancestor Jacob, who gave us this well? How can you offer better water than he and his sons and his animals enjoyed?" 13 Jesus replied, "Anyone who drinks this water will soon become thirsty again. 14 But those who drink the water I give will never be thirsty again. It becomes a fresh, bubbling spring within them, giving them eternal life." 15 "Please, sir," the woman said, "give me this water! Then I'll never be thirsty again, and I won't have to come here to get water."

Drinking Spiritual Water: John 4:14 NLT
But those who drink the water I give will never be thirsty again. It becomes a fresh, bubbling spring within them, giving them eternal life."

The Sheep and the Goats: Matthew 25:32-40 NIV
32 All nations will be gathered before Him, and He will separate the people one from another as a shepherd separates the sheep from the goats. 33 He will put the sheep on his right and the goats on his left. 34 "Then the King will say to those on his right, 'Come, you who are blessed by my Father; take your inheritance, the kingdom prepared for you since the creation of the world. 35 For I was hungry and you gave me something to eat, I was thirsty and you gave me something to drink, I was a stranger and you invited me in, 36 I needed clothes and you clothed me, I was sick and you looked after me, I was in prison and you came to visit me.'
37 "Then the righteous will answer him, 'Lord, when did we see you hungry and feed you, or thirsty and give you something to drink? 38 When did we see you a stranger and invite you in, or needing clothes and clothe you? 39

When did we see you sick or in prison and go to visit you?'
40 "The King will reply, 'Truly I tell you, whatever you did for one of the least of these brothers and sisters of mine, you did for me.'

Rewarding to Serve: Matthew 10:42 NLT
And whoever gives one of these little ones even a cup of cold water because he is a disciple, truly, I say to you, he will by no means lose his reward."

Notes:

Notes: